BIBLIOTHECA HIBERNICANA

BIBLIOTHECA HIBERNICANA

or
a Descriptive Catalogue of a
Select Irish Library
collected for
the Right Hon Robert Peel

with an Essay by
NORMAN D PALMER

IRISH UNIVERSITY PRESS
Shannon · Ireland

First edition 1823

Essay by Norman D Palmer first published in
Irish Historical Studies Vol·VI, No 22, September 1948

This IUP reprint is a photolithographic facsimile of
the first edition and is unabridged even to the extent
of retaining the original printer's imprint

Microforms

Microfilm, microfiche and other forms of micro-publishing
© *Irish University Microforms Shannon Ireland*

SBN 7165 0022 1

Irish University Press Shannon Ireland
DUBLIN CORK BELFAST LONDON NEW YORK
T M MacGlinchey Publisher

PRINTED IN THE REPUBLIC OF IRELAND AT SHANNON
BY ROBERT HOGG PRINTER TO IRISH UNIVERSITY PRESS

Sir Robert Peel's 'Select Irish library'

While in Ireland as chief secretary (1812–18), Sir Robert Peel became acquainted with William Shaw Mason, the Irish topographer and statistician who was remembrancer or receiver of the first-fruits or twentieth parts in Ireland and secretary to the commissioners for public records. Impressed with Mason's work and abilities, Peel encouraged him to prepare a major statistical survey of Ireland, along the lines of Sir John Sinclair's famous survey of Scotland;[1] and the result was the three-volume work entitled *A statistical account, or parochial survey of Ireland, drawn up from the communications of the clergy* (the three volumes were published in 1814, 1816, and 1819 respectively), which is still a valuable record of the period. In 1819 Mason compiled a *Survey, valuation, and census of the barony of Portnehinch* in Queen's County. Published in 1821, this work was submitted to George IV during the royal visit to Ireland in that year ' as a model for a statistical survey of the whole country '.[2]

At about the same time Mason was engaged on another project for Sir Robert Peel. The chief secretary had perforce become much concerned with Irish affairs, and had devoted considerable attention to collecting tracts of all kinds on Ireland. To supplement this collection, Peel asked Mason to assemble for him ' a select Irish library '. Mason approached the task ' with all care and anxiety ', seeking ' to afford general views of the circumstances of the country ' and to include ' the principal writers on the leading subjects and events of the several periods, from the earliest extant to the year 1820 '. The result was an outstanding collection of some 170 volumes, ' uniformly bound in green Morocco ', to grace Sir Robert's library.

[1] *The statistical account of Scotland, drawn up from the communications of the ministers of the different parishes* (21 vols, Edinburgh, 1791–9).
[2] *D.N.B.*, s.v. Mason.

In 1823 fifty copies of the catalogue of this collection were published in Dublin by W. Folds and Son, under the title *Bibliotheca Hibernicana: or a descriptive catalogue of a select Irish library, collected for the Right Hon. Robert Peel.*[3] The volumes which Mason selected were listed under seven main headings : ' Antiquities ', ' History ', ' Biography ', ' Topography ', ' Statistical Surveys ', ' Tourists ', and ' Finance '; there were 125 separate entries (some referring to more than one work), with valuable comments on each item and brief notes about the authors.   The headings suggest that the collection was weighted heavily in favour of the compiler's own interests; as a matter of fact, over one-third of the volumes are listed under 'Topography' or 'Statistical Surveys'.   Some items which to-day would be classified as ' Literature ' are included under ' Antiquities ' or ' History '.   Editions of the great Irish annals and genealogies are represented chiefly by Vallancey's *Collectanea*; but, of course, critical editions of the great classics were still lacking.   Giraldus Cambrensis, Edmund Campion, John Colgan, Geoffrey Keating, the Four Masters, and other great names are not represented in the catalogue by separate works.   Although the first volume of the Reverend Charles O'Conor's important, if inaccurate, *Rerum Hibernicarum scriptores veteres* was published in 1814, it does not appear on Mason's list.   No reference is included to the *Transactions of the Royal Irish Academy,* the first volume of which appeared in 1787.

After all necessary reservations are made, however, the fact remains that this rare and interesting catalogue of a ' select Irish library ', compiled by a qualified authority for a man who was to become one of the great English statesmen of the nineteenth century, offers a concise summary of many of the most significant works on Ireland that had appeared up to 1820, and is made doubly valuable by the observations of the compiler. An analysis of the items listed in this catalogue of 1823 should, therefore, be illuminating.

[3] The exact number and location of the copies of this catalogue still extant could not be determined.   Among libraries now possessing a copy are the National Library of Ireland, the Royal Irish Academy, the British Museum, and the Library of Congress.   There are some notes on *Bibliotheca Hibernicana* in *I.B.L.,* ii. 182, 196; vii. 117.

Quite appropriately, the first item in the catalogue is the first English edition of some of the works of 'the Camden of Ireland', Sir James Ware (1594–1666), under the title *Antiquities and history of Ireland* (London, 1705). To Ware, says Kenney, 'is mainly due the introduction of Irish history as a subject of scholarly interest to the English-speaking world'.[4] The husband of Ware's great-granddaughter, Walter Harris, edited two volumes of a projected three-volume translation of Ware's writings, *The whole works of Sir James Ware concerning Ireland, revised and improved* (2 vols, Dublin, 1739, 1745–6[5]), and these volumes are also included in Mason's list.

The next items are three works on the antiquities of Ireland by Wright, Grose, and Ledwich,[6] published in 1748, 1791, and 1803 respectively; Mervyn Archdall's *Monasticon Hibernicum* (Dublin, 1786); two works by Joseph C. Walker on Irish bards and Irish dress, published in 1786 and 1788 respectively;[7] Charlotte Brooke's *Reliques of Irish poetry* (Dublin, 1789), a remarkable book of translations from original Irish poems, with the original texts included, which, according to Desmond Ryan, 'brought the folk-songs of Ireland into English once and for all';[8] a history of the Dominican order in Ireland by de Burgo (Kilkenny, 1762); and Richard Stanyhurst's *De rebus in Hibernia gestis*, published in 1584.[9] A book on epitaphs by O'Phelan and one on Irish coins by Simon, both published in the early nineteenth century, concluded Mason's selections of 'Antiquaries'.

[4] Kenney, *Sources*, p. 48.

[5] 'The unsold copies of Harris's edition of Ware's writings were reissued at Dublin with new title-pages in 1764' (*D.N.B.*, s.v. Harris). Mason lists this edition of 1764.

[6] Edward Ledwich gained much notoriety by his bold denial of the very existence of St Patrick. William Shaw Mason, *Bibliotheca Hibernicana*, p. 3.

[7] Mason's date for the publication of the two volumes (1764) does not agree with the dates given by the *D.N.B.* or by Kenney (*Sources*, p. 59).

[8] *The sword of light; from the Four Masters to Douglas Hyde, 1636–1938* (London, 1939), p. 52.

[9] It is hard to understand why the history of Ireland by Stanyhurst's more famous friend, Edmund Campion, was not also selected as a separate item by Mason.

The history section of the catalogue is very rich.   It includes
Sir John Davies' *Discoverie of the true causes why Ireland was
never entirely subdued, nor brought under obedience to the
crowne of England, untill the beginning of His Majesties happie
raigne* (London, 1612); and the general works of Sir Richard
Cox (2 vols, Dublin, 1689); Ferdinando Warner (London,
1763)); Sylvester O'Halloran[10] (Dublin, 1772); Thomas Leland
(3 vols, London, 1773), whose work, highly praised on its
appearance, was soon subjected to devastating criticism; James
Macpherson (London, 1773), celebrated translator of the
pseudo-Ossianic poems, whose publication ' marks a great
moment in the history of Celtic literature ',[11] and ushered in a
violent controversy over the Milesian origin of the Irish;
Thomas Campbell (Dublin, 1789), who shared Macpherson's
views; and Francis Plowden (3 vols, London, 1803).   Mason
also lists Sir Richard Musgrave's criticism of Plowden's history[12]
(London, 1804), and the accounts of the controversy between
Plowden and the Reverend Charles O'Conor over the method
of appointing catholic bishops in Ireland.[13]   Two contemporary
narratives of the last years of Elizabeth's reign, published at
later dates by Fynes Moryson, secretary to Lord Mountjoy,
lord deputy of Ireland (*The history of Ireland, from 1599 to
1603,* 2 vols, Dublin, 1735), and by Sir George Carew, president
of Munster (*Pacata Hibernia,* 2 vols, Dublin, 1810), were
selected by Mason, as was Lodge's *Desiderata curiosa Hibernica*
(2 vols, Dublin, 1772), a miscellaneous collection of state papers
and historical tracts of the late sixteenth and early seventeenth

[10] O'Halloran, reports Desmond Ryan, ' maintained that Irish had
been spoken by Japhet, and before that son of Noah in Paradise itself '
(*The sword of light,* p. 75).

[11] Dr Magnus MacLean, quoted by Eoin MacNeill in *Phases of
Irish History* (Dublin, 1918), p. 8.

[12] But Mason does not give equal attention to Plowden's replies to
Musgrave (*A postliminious preface to the historical review of the state
of Ireland* (London, 1804), and *An historical letter to Sir Richard
Musgrave, Bart.* (London, 1805), although he does refer to the latter
work in his comments on Musgrave's book.   See article on Plowden in
D.N.B.

[13] O'Conor's *Columbanus ad Hibernos* (2 vols, London, 1810–13),
and Plowden's *An historical letter to C. O'Conor, D.D., heretofore
styling himself Columbanus* (Dublin, 1812).

centuries.   Also listed were Walter Harris's *Hibernica; or some antient pieces relating to Ireland* (Dublin, 1757); a reprint in 1809 of the *Historie of Ireland* edited by Sir James Ware in 1633, containing the famous descriptions of Ireland by Edmund Campion, Meredith Hanmer, Henry of Marlborough, and Edmund Spenser; and Bishop William Nicolson's *Irish Historical Library* (Dublin, 1724), which, according to Mason, ' may be considered as the best preparatory book for the study of Irish history ',[14] and which is still of value to-day.

Special mention should be made of Charles Vallancey's *Collectanea de rebus Hibernicis* (6 vols, 1770–1804);[15] in this collection Vallancey, ' an English military engineer of French Protestant parentage ', who, though ' in almost complete ignorance of the original sources ' and addicted to the wildest theories, ' for the first time published texts and translations of early Irish literary and historical sources ' and ' contributed very much to the advancement of Irish studies '.[16]

Three entries in the catalogue recall the work of the great Charles O'Conor of Belanagare (1710–91), ' the most valuable servant Irish history had in the eighteenth century ' :[17] his *Dissertations on the ancient history of Ireland* (Dublin, 1753); his edition of Roderic O'Flaherty's *Ogygia vindicated* [18] (Dublin, 1775), a work which in Mason's opinion is ' necessary for every person desirous of becoming acquainted with the early history and chronology of Ireland ';[19] and *Memoirs of the life and writings of the late Charles O'Conor of Belanagare, Esq.* by his grandson, the Reverend Charles O'Conor (Dublin, 1796). Mason reported that this last book was ' very scarce ', even in 1823, and a copy would command a high price to-day.   The

[14] *Bibliotheca Hibernicana*, p. 9.

[15] Mason erroneously states that this compilation ' was commenced in 1774 ' (ibid., p. 13).   The first number was published in 1770 and the whole project, as the editor stated in his preface to the first number, embodied ' the fruit of many years research '.

[16] Kenney, *Sources,* pp. 58–9; see also Ryan, *The sword of light,* pp. 74–5.

[17] Kenney, *Sources,* p. 56.

[18] O'Flaherty's *Ogygia seu rerum Hibernicarum chronologia* was published in London in 1685.

[19] *Bibliotheca Hibernicana*, p. 13.

first volume of a projected two-volume study was suppressed soon after publication, apparently to prevent embarrassment to O'Conor's family; and the second volume was burned 'at the author's particular request'.[20]

Mason's historical section also includes two studies, by Parnell and Scully (published in 1808 and 1812 respectively), of the penal laws, and four rather curious volumes on the Irish parliament. One of these covers more ground than its title [21] would indicate, and even contains Giraldus Cambrensis's account of the invasion of Ireland in an appendix. Two others by 'Falkland' (pseudonym of John Robert Scott) deal with membership and representation in the Irish parliament in the late eighteenth century. The fourth study has the intriguing title of *Pou-Rou, or an historical and critical inquiry into the physiology and pathology of parliaments* (Dublin, 1786).

The absence of standard Irish histories of the early nineteenth century, notably Francis Plowden's *The history of Ireland from its union with Great Britain, in January, 1801, to October 1810* (3 vols, Dublin, 1811), is explained by Mason's decision to make the date of the Act of Union the terminal point for his historical collection.[22]

'Biography' is represented in the catalogue by only five titles: Thomas Carte's life of the duke of Ormond (1610–88), in three volumes (London, 1735–6), the third volume containing a collection of letters and papers relating to English and Irish affairs from 1640 to 1660; Francis Hardy's life of the earl of Charlemont (2 vols, London, 1810[23]), the leader of the Volunteers; Richard Rawlinson's edition (London, 1728) of *The history of that most eminent statesman, Sir John Perrott, . . . lord lieutenant of Ireland,* a document written toward the end of Elizabeth's reign; Sheffield Grace's *Memoirs of the family of Grace* (London, 1823), a rare volume, illustrated with some fifty engravings, 'intended solely for private distri-

---

[20] *Bibliotheca Hibernicana,* p. 12.
[21] *The history of the principal transactions of the Irish parliament from . . . 1634 to 1666,* by Henry Redmond Morres, 2nd viscount Mountmorres (2 vols, London, 1792).
[22] *Bibliotheca Hibernicana,* p. 18, n. 1.
[23] Mason lists the second edition (2 vols, London, 1812).

bution', which Mason calls 'the most curious account extant in print of any private family in the kingdom';[24] and John Lodge's famous *Peerage of Ireland,* edited and continued by Mervyn Archdall (7 vols, Dublin, 1789[25]).

In his preface Mason confessed that he departed from his principles of selection in his listings on 'Topography', and because of his intimate knowledge of and particular interest in the subject endeavored to make this section ' as complete as the materials would allow '. General works included two valuable topographical dictionaries, by Seward and Carlisle, published in Dublin in 1795 and 1810 respectively; Beaufort's *Memoir of a map of Ireland* (2 vols, London, 1792); a 1755 reprint of Molyneux's edition (Dublin, 1726) of Gerard Boate's classic work on *Irelands naturall history,* first published in 1652, with a ' discourse concerning the Danish mounts, forts, and towers in Ireland ' by the editor; and an interesting tract on *The present state of Ireland,* published in London in 1673. Even in 1823 this tract was ' scarce and valuable ', and it is now a collector's item. It is also noteworthy for a strange old map of Ireland which it contains.

Several town and county histories are listed in this section, including Hardiman's history of Galway (Dublin, 1820), which is generally regarded as a classic in its field; histories of Dublin by Walter Harris (Dublin, 1766), containing two plans of the city, one for 1610 (the earliest extant plan) and the other for 1766, and by Warburton, Whitelaw, and Walsh (2 vols, London, 1818), which was begun as an enlargement of Harris's work;[26] a history of Down (Dublin, 1744), probably written by Walter

[24] *Bibliotheca Hibernicana,* p. 21.

[25] Mason gives the date as 1788. The first edition of Lodge's work, in four volumes, was published in London in 1754.

[26] These two histories of Dublin were notoriously inaccurate, for reasons explained by Sir John T. Gilbert in his article on Walter Harris in the *D.N.B.* : ' Some imperfect and inaccurate papers left by Harris came into the possession of a Dublin book-dealer, who, in 1766, printed them with the title of the " History and Antiquities of the City of Dublin " (also London, 1766). Much of this work was reprinted, without acknowledgment and with additional errors, in " A History of the City of Dublin," by Whitelaw and Walsh, London 1818.'

Harris and Charles Smith; [27] histories of Waterford (Dublin, 1746), Cork (Dublin, 1749), and Kerry [28] (Dublin, 1756) by Charles Smith; [29] Ferrar's history of Limerick (Limerick, 1787); McSkimin's history of Carrickfergus (Belfast, 1811); Stuart's history of Armagh [30] (Newry, 1819), and a collection of historical materials relating to Belfast (Belfast, 1817).

In a class by itself among the topographical works is a scarce production of two artists, Robert Poole and John Cash, entitled *Views of the most remarkable public buildings, monuments and other edifices in the city of Dublin* (Dublin, 1780), which has great historical and architectural value.   It contains plans of

[27] Mason stated positively that this work was written 'by Walter Harris and Dr Lyons, and was the first work published under the auspices of the Physico-Historical Society' (*Bibliotheca Hibernicana*, p. 25).   Sir John T. Gilbert, in his article on Harris in the *D.N.B.*, merely states that 'In 1744 Harris helped the Physico-Historical Society of Dublin to produce "The ancient and present state of the county of Down"'.   However, C. Litton Falkiner, in his article on Charles Smith in the *D.N.B.*, definitely attributes the work to Harris and Smith : 'In 1744 he [Smith] published, in conjunction with Walter Harris, . . . a history of the county Down.   This was the first Irish county history on a large scale ever written.   The preface to this book contains the outline of a plan for a series of Irish county histories, which appears to have led in 1744 to his foundation at Dublin of the Physico-Historical Society for the purpose of providing topographical materials for such a series.'   The British Museum catalogue lists the book under the name of Walter Harris, with a question mark.   The Library of Congress catalogue attributes it to Harris and Smith.   Mason lists the edition of 1757, instead of 1744.

[28] According to Mason. this is 'the scarcest of Smith's works' (*Bibliotheca Hibernicana*, p. 26).

[29] The importance of Smith's county histories may be judged by the following comments of C. Litton Falkiner : 'Although encumbered with much irrelevant ·matter, these volumes form a valuable contribution to Irish topography, of which Smith may be regarded as the pioneer. Smith's statements of fact are generally to be trusted, though it was said of him in the counties of which he was the historian that his descriptions were regulated by the reception he was given in the houses he visited while making his investigations.   His books were warmly commended by Macaulay, who frequently refers to them in his "History"'   *D.N.B.*

[30] This interesting work, by James Stuart (Mason spells his name 'Stewart'), purported to cover the history of Armagh 'for a period of 1373 years', and also included, for good measure, 'a refutation of the opinions of Dr Ledwich, respecting the non-existence of St Patrick'.

Dublin in 1610 and 1780.[31]   Among other specialized topographical studies Mason selected Patterson's treatise on the
climate of Ireland (Dublin, 1804); Barton's lectures on Lough
Neagh (Dublin, 1751); two surveys by the eminent statistician,
Sir Richard Griffith, of the coal districts of Leinster and
Connacht, published in 1814 and 1818 respectively; and three
works of an eighteenth-century Quaker physician and amateur
scientist, John Rutty, on mineral waters (Dublin, 1757), on ' the
weather and seasons ' and ' the prevailing diseases ' of Dublin
(London, 1770), and on the natural history of the county of
Dublin (Dublin, 1772).

Under the heading ' Statistical Surveys ' were listed many
famous works which are much more comprehensive in scope
than the heading would suggest.   Perhaps the most noteworthy
were Sir William Petty's *Political tracts, chiefly relating to
Ireland* (Dublin, 1769), containing *A discourse of taxes and
contributions, Political arithmetic,* and *The political anatomy of
Ireland,* ' certainly one of the first and most valuable statistical
documents respecting the country '.[32]   Equally well-known is
Arthur Young's *Tour in Ireland* (London, 1780), based on
careful observations made during visits to Ireland in 1776, 1777,
1778, and 1779.   ' This work ', stated Mason, ' may be
considered as the first and among the best of the treatises on
the agricultural state of Ireland '.[33]   It had a considerable effect
on the course of Irish political and economic development and,
as Dr Constantia Maxwell has remarked, ' has certainly " stood
its ground " in that it remains our chief authority for Irish
economic conditions for the latter part of the eighteenth
century '.[34]

The other general works in this section were recognized in
the early nineteenth century as standard treatises.   Especially
important are two books by Thomas Newenham, *A statistical
and historical inquiry into the progress and magnitude of the*

[31] For some reason, these plans were not included in all the copies of
this work.   A perfect copy, with the plans, would therefore be doubly
valuable.

[32] *Bibliotheca Hibernicana,* p. 39.

[33] Ibid., p. 32.

[34] Arthur Young, *A tour in Ireland,* ed. Constantia Maxwell
(Cambridge, 1925), p. xv.

population of Ireland (London, 1805) and *A view of the natural, political and commercial circumstances of Ireland* (London, 1809); the two surveys by the compiler of the *Bibliotheca Hibernicana* which have already been described in the introduction to this paper; and Edward Wakefield's *An account of Ireland, statistical and political* (2 vols, London, 1812), which, though often inaccurate and poorly organized, is a mine of information on Irish matters.

Between 1802 and 1812 twenty-one county surveys were published under the auspices of the Dublin Society,[35] with the aid of a special parliamentary grant, and all of these are listed by Mason. A complete set of these surveys would be a valuable collection for any library. Naturally the volumes varied in quality. Some were considered to be disappointing, even by the critical standards of a century and a quarter ago, but others were outstanding, particularly those for Cork, Kilkenny, and Londonderry.[36] The survey of Meath, prepared by Robert Thompson (Dublin, 1802), was, according to Mason, 'the scarcest of all the Surveys'.[37]

Many of the twenty-six works listed under 'Tourists' can still be read with delight. The first of the tourists, in Mason's opinion, was John Dunton (1659–1733), who in 1699 printed a book bearing the curious title of *The Dublin Scuffle: a challenge sent by John Dunton, citizen of London, to Patrick Campbell, bookseller in Dublin. . . . to which is added some account of his conversation in Ireland*, which 'may be considered as the earliest attempt at Irish topography'.[38]   The next in

[35] The Dublin Society was founded in 1731 and incorporated in 1750 as the 'Dublin Society for promoting husbandry and other useful arts in Ireland'. A royal charter was granted in 1820, when its name was changed to the Royal Dublin Society.

[36] *Bibliotheca Hibernicana*, p. 33.   [37] Ibid., p. 35.

[38] Ibid., p. 42. Alexander Pope thus referred to Dunton in the *Dunciad* (Book II):

> With that she gave him (piteous of his case,
> Yet smiling at his rueful length of face)
> A shaggy tap'stry, worthy to be spread
> On Codrus' old, or Dunton's modern bed.

In a footnote to this passage in the 1729 edition of the *Dunciad,* Pope called Dunton 'a broken bookseller and abusive scribbler'. Whitwell Elwin and William J. Courthope, *The works of Alexander Pope* (London, 1882), iv. 140.

chronological order was Chetwood's *A tour through Ireland*
(London, 1746), which, despite the title, described the south-
eastern part of the country only.   Other important accounts are
Hibernia curiosa (London, 1768 ?), the record of a journey
from Dublin to Killarney and elsewhere in 1764 by John Bush;[38a]
Elstob's *A trip to Kilkenny . . . in the year 1776* (Dublin, 1779);
*Letters written from Liverpool, Chester, Corke, the Lake of
Killarney, etc.* (2 vols, Dublin, 1767) by Samuel Derrick, the
poet and dramatist who was Beau Nash's successor at Bath;
A tour in Ireland (London, 1776) by Richard Twiss, who ' has
been " damned to everlasting fame " for some severe remarks
on the Irish ladies ';[39] *A philosophical survey of the south of
Ireland* (London, 1777[40]) by Thomas Campbell, author of
Strictures on the ecclesiastical history of Ireland, who ' has
always been considered as among the best of the Irish tourists ';[41]
Cooper's *Letters on the Irish nation in the year 1799* (London,
1801); de Latocnaye's *Promenade du francois dans l'Irlande*
(Brunswick, 1801; a translation by John Stevenson was published
in Belfast in 1917), an entertaining narrative of a walking tour
through Ireland in 1796–7; Isaac Weld's *Illustrations of the
scenery of Killarney* (London, 1807), an attractive book which
' should form part of the travelling equipage of every visitor
in these romantic scenes ';[42] Sir John Carr's *The stranger in
Ireland; or a tour in the southern and western parts of that
country in the year 1805* (London, 1806), a book that is pompous

---

[38a] Mason gives 1764 as the date of publication.   No date is given
on the title-page, but the conclusion of the 143-page letter reads : ' I am,
dear sir, With great esteem, Your affectionate, humble servant, J. B.
Lucas's Coffee-house, Dublin, 30th Novemb. 1764 '.   Apparently, however, the book was published in or about 1768.   The catalogues of the
British Museum and of the Library of Congress give this year, with a
question-mark; Robert Watt's *Bibliotheca Britannica* (vol. i, Edinburgh,
1824) gives 1767.   Another edition was published in London in 1769.

[39] *Bibliotheca Hibernica,* p. 44.   The *D.N.B.* states that Twiss's book
' was very unpopular in Ireland '.

[40] Mason lists the edition published in Dublin in 1778.

[41] *Bibliotheca Hibernicana,* p. 44.   On pages 437–8 of Campbell's
work Dr Johnson's epitaph on Oliver Goldsmith appears for the first
time in print.   In spite of the title there is ' not much philosophy in
this book ' (*D.N.B.*).

[42] *Bibliotheca Hibernicana,* p. 41.

both in style and in approach;[43] *Journal of a tour in Ireland,
A.D. 1806* (London, 1807[44]) by Sir Richard Colt Hoare, a
well-known antiquarian; Daniel Dewar's *Observations on the
character, customs, and superstitions of the Irish* (London,
1812), an interesting account by a friendly Scottish visitor;
Atkinson's *Irish Tourist* (Dublin, 1815), a ' laborious compilation ';[45] *Observations on the state of Ireland* (2 vols,
London, 1818) by John C. Curwen, an English agriculturist,
based on a hasty visit to Ireland in 1815; *The scientific tourist
through Ireland* (London, 1818), a meaty county-by-county
survey by Thomas Walford; and *Walks through Ireland in the
years 1812, 1814, and 1817* (London, 1819), by John Bernard
Trotter, who had been private secretary to Charles James Fox.

The last section, headed ' Finance ', has only five entries:
a seventeenth-century work by Colonel Richard Lawrence, *The
interest of Ireland in its trade and wealth stated* (Dublin, 1682);
The commercial restraints of Ireland considered (Dublin, 1779)
by John Hely-Hutchinson, the famous Irish political leader and
provost of Trinity College, a strong propagandist tract designed
to show the evils resulting from the economic restrictions
imposed upon Ireland by Great Britain; Clarendon's *A sketch
of the revenues and finances of Ireland* (London, 1791);
Cavendish's *A statement of the public accounts of Ireland*
(London, 1791); and a valuable work by George Chalmers
entitled *An historical view of the domestic economy of Great
Britain and Ireland, from the earliest to the present times*
(Edinburgh, 1812), containing a chapter which reviews Irish
economic and political development from 1603 to 1801.[46]

Aside from serving as a check-list of important Irish works
which were published before 1820, an analysis of *Bibliotheca
Hibernicana* inevitably calls attention to its indefatigable
compiler, who deserves to be remembered for his solid surveys
and for his services to the Public Records Commission, and to

[43] It was cleverly satirized by Edward Dubois in a book entitled
My pocket book; or, hints for ' A righte merrie and conceited' tour . . .
by a knight errant (Dublin, 1808).

[44] Mason cites an edition of 1810.

[45] *Bibliotheca Hibernicana,* p. 48.

[46] This chapter was not included in the first edition of Chalmers's
book, published in 1804 (*Bibliotheca Hibernicana,* p. 51).

a number of almost-forgotten studies which still have a considerable value for Irish antiquarians.   And, finally, the rarity of
many of the books on Mason's list should be a challenge and
a stimulus to private collectors and the literary sleuths of the
larger libraries.   Who knows into what interesting labyrinths
the search for these precious stones of another day may not
lead?

NORMAN D. PALMER

For there is no Nation of People vnder the Sun, that doth Love æquall, and indifferent Justice, better then the Irish, or will rest better satisfied w: the execution thereof, although it bee against themselves; So as they may have the protection and benefitt of the Lawe, wh: vppon iust cause they doe desire it.

For, there is
no Nation of people vnder the sunne,
that doth loue equall and indifferent
Iustice, better then the Irish: or will
rest better satisfied with the execution thereof, although it bee against
themselues; so as they may haue the
protection & benefit of the Law,
when vppon iust cause
they do desire
it.

FINIS.

BIBLIOTHECA HIBERNICANA:

OR A

𝔇𝔢𝔰𝔠𝔯𝔦𝔭𝔱𝔦𝔟𝔢 ℭ𝔞𝔱𝔞𝔩𝔬𝔤𝔲𝔢

OF A

SELECT IRISH LIBRARY,

COLLECTED FOR

THE RIGHT HON. ROBERT PEEL,

&c. &c. &c.

" Attamen audendum est et veritas investiganda," &c.
Shaw Mason's Parochial Survey of Ireland.

" For not to be able to find what we know to be in our possession, is a
" more vexatious circumstance, than the mere want of what we have
" neglected to procure. This Catalogue will not only assist the forgetful,
" but direct the inquisitive."
Dr. Johnson.

DUBLIN:

PRINTED BY W. FOLDS AND SON,

GREAT STRAND-STREET.

1823.

In forming the selection of Works upon Irish affairs to which this Catalogue refers, the compiler intended to afford general views of the circumstances of the country, without embarrassing the reader with a multiplicity of details; it contains, therefore, the principal writers on the leading subjects and events of the several periods, from the earliest extant to the year 1820, classed under the following heads :— ANTIQUITIES, HISTORY, BIOGRAPHY, TOPOGRAPHY, STATISTICAL SURVEYS, TOURISTS, and FINANCE.

This was not, however, the only motive which actuated the compiler in his choice. The collection itself has been formed with all the care and anxiety, which a deep sense of many obligations conferred upon him could excite. The enlightened individual for whom this pleasing task was undertaken with every sentiment of gratitude and respectful attachment, had, during his residence in this country as Chief Secretary, devoted some of his valuable time to collecting Tracts on Irish affairs. It was, therefore, only necessary to fill up the vacant spaces in this department of literature. The sole exception to the principle of selection here stated is in the department of Topography, in which the compiler's favorite pursuits have led him to a deviation from his general rule, by making this department of the Select Irish Library as complete as the materials would allow.

He has endeavoured to give an additional interest to the Catalogue, by the insertion of short bibliographical notes, collected as well from private sources, as from printed authorities. The present attempt, perhaps, would not have been made, had he not been able to avail himself of the assistance of a literary friend, who is now engaged in preparing a similar Work, on a much more extended scale, being designed to

comprehend whatever ha. been written upon
Ireland, so as to form a complete Irish Historical
Library; a work of much labour and research,
and to the completion of which, he is not
without hopes that this *prelusion* may have given
a stimulus.

The collection consisting of 125 numbers,
is uniformly bound in green Morocco. The
series of authors is brought down to the year
1820, at which time the collection was made;
with the exception of the Memoirs of the
Grace Family, and of the Model of the Royal
Statistical Survey, both of which, having been
since introduced into the Library, are conse-
quently described in the Catalogue.

W. S. M.

RECORD TOWER,
    DUBLIN CASTLE;
        September, 1823.

CONTENTS.

———

ANTIQUITIES.

1. **𝕎are's** ANTIQUITIES AND HISTORY OF IRELAND. *London,* 1705. *Folio.*

Bishop Nicholson calls Sir James Ware " the Camden of Ireland;" adding, " that this kingdom " is everlastingly obliged for the great pains which " he took, in collecting and preserving our scat- " tered monuments of antiquity." This is the first English edition.

* **ℌarris's** EDITION OF WARE. *Dublin,* 1764. *2 vols. Folio.*

Walter Harris, who was among the first, and certainly among the most able of the members of the Physico-Historical Society of Dublin, formed for investigating the ancient state of Ireland, undertook a new edition of Ware's works, which he designed to publish in three volumes. The first two only were printed: they contain the Antiquities, the Lives of the Bishops, and the Irish

Writers continued to the beginning of the 18th century. He did not live to complete the third, which was to comprehend the Annals of Ireland. A most valuable Collectanea for this purpose, consisting of several closely written folios, was purchased by the late Irish Parliament, and is deposited in the library of the Dublin Society.

2. Grose's Antiquities of Ireland. *Large Paper.* London, 1791. 4*to*.

Commenced by Grose, the celebrated antiquary, and continued by his nephew, Lieutenant Grose. It is principally valuable for its engravings, mostly executed from drawings collected by the late Right Honorable William Burton Conyngham. The historical and descriptive parts were written by Dr. Ledwich, the Irish antiquary, who has also enriched it by an introduction to the pagan, monastic, and military antiquities of Ireland.

3. Wright's Louthiana; or an Introduction to the Antiquities of Ireland. London, 1748. 4*to*.

The commencement of an attempt to illustrate the antiquities of Ireland, which, however, proceeded no further than the present volume, comprehending the county of Louth.

4. **Ledwich's** Antiquities of Ireland.
Dublin, 1803. 4*to.*

The origin of this work may be traced in Vallancey's Collectanea. A difference of opinion arose between these learned writers as to the primeval inhabitants of Ireland, which was long carried on with much spirit, not altogether untinctured with acrimony. Ledwich argues against his antagonist's hypothesis of the Eastern or Phenician descent of the Irish, and boldly denies the existence of St. Patrick. Hence it may be easily inferred, that he is no favorite with the majority of Irish antiquarians.

5. **Archdall's** Monasticon Hibernicum.
Dublin, 1786. 4*to.*

The history of Irish monastic institutions was originally composed by Allemande, who wrote a small treatise, in French, on the subject, chiefly drawn from Ware's works. It was published in Paris, and afterwards appeared in an English dress, somewhat enlarged, in 1722. The present work rests on the same foundation, but is considerably augmented from the records, and other sources of information.

6. **Walker's** Irish Bards and Dresses.
Dublin, 1764. *2 vols.* 4*to.*

A work of taste and ingenuity, but not displaying much erudition or knowledge of Irish antiquities.

7. 𝕭𝖗𝖔𝖔𝖐𝖊'𝖘 RELICS OF IRISH POETRY. *Dublin,* 1789. 4*to.*

Miss Brooke, the author of this selection of translations from original Irish Poems, was the daughter of Henry Brooke, esq. who wrote several tracts on the political occurrences of Ireland during his own time, but is best known as author of The Fool of Quality, and the tragedy of Gustavus Vasa. Her translations, though written in a pleasing style, are far from conveying the wild and romantic spirit of the originals.

8. 𝕭𝖚𝖗𝖌𝖍'𝖘 HIBERNIA DOMINICANA CUM SUPPLEMENTO. *Kilk.* 1762. 4*to.*

This work, though most of the copies bear the imprint of " Cologne," was executed by Edmund Finn, at Kilkenny, under Burgh's own inspection. It contains a full account of the origin and state of the Dominican order in Ireland. The supplement, printed in 1772, was intended to vindicate Rinucini, the pope's nuncio, from the charges forwarded to Rome against him by the confederate Catholics of Ireland. The work was publicly censured by several Roman Catholic clergy, for containing principles inimical to the allegiance of Catholics to Protestant states; and is at present difficult to be procured in a perfect state, as that part of it containing the reign of James II. has been carefully cancelled in most copies.

9. 𝕾𝖙𝖆𝖓𝖎𝖍𝖚𝖗𝖘𝖙 DE REBUS IN HIBERNIA. *Ludg.* 1584. *4to.*

This work, the author of which was the son of a recorder of Dublin, also appears in an English form. The present is the original edition. Keating, the Irish historian, falls foul of this book, and represents it as the production of a prejudiced writer; but Bishop Nicholson says, that, waving some little digressions, it must be confessed that what he writes concerning the manners and language of the inhabitants, and the strength and traffic of their chief cities, the antiquities and achievements of their prime nobility, &c. is highly commendable.

10. 𝕺'𝕻𝖍𝖊𝖑𝖆𝖓'𝖘 EPITAPHS. *Dublin,* 1813: *Folio.*

A curious account of some antique reliques, chiefly monumental, found in the cathedral church of St. Canice, Kilkenny.

11. 𝕾𝖎𝖒𝖔𝖓'𝖘 ESSAY ON IRISH COINS. *Reprinted with Snelling. London,* 1810. *4to.*

A standard work on Irish numismatics, written about the year 1750. Snelling's additions are useful, though not numerous.

HISTORY.

12. Cox's History of Ireland. *Dublin,* 1689. *2 vols. Folio.*

From the English conquest to the Revolution. It consists of two parts, or volumes; the first affording annals to the end of the reign of Elizabeth, the second, an account of the subsequent period, in rather a hasty and desultory manner. Walter Harris tells us, that judicious writers have looked on Sir Richard Cox only in the light of an annalist; adding, that we have not in him what may be called a general history of Ireland. He says there are vast chasms in several reigns, which might have been filled up from the record office; but he has furnished the world with some good materials out of the Lambeth library.

13. M'Pherson's Introduction to the History of Great Britain and Ireland. *London,* 1773. *4to.*

This is the work of the celebrated translator of Ossian, and seems to have been undertaken with the view of giving the colour of historical truth to the narratives contained in those beautiful compositions. The writer controverts the Milesian origin of the Irish, asserting that the inhabitants of those islands were of Scotch descent, and concludes with an introductory essay on the history of the Anglo-Saxons. He is not to be confounded with James M'Pherson, author of Critical Dissertations on the Origin of the Ancient Caledonians.

14. **O'Halloran's** INTRODUCTION TO THE STUDY AND ANTIQUITIES OF IRELAND. *Dublin*, 1772. *4to.*

The author was born in Limerick, where he was very eminent in the profession of medicine. It appears by several of his works, that he was not only skilful in his profession, but learned in the Irish language and ancient laws, and a warm advocate for the honour and interest of his native country. Besides this introduction, he has also published a general history of Ireland from the earliest accounts to the close of the 12th century.

15. **Warner's** HISTORY OF IRELAND. *London*, 1763. *4to.*

Warner, the author of this work, also wrote the history of the Irish rebellion, in quarto, published in 1767, for which his candour has been praised by Plowden, and other writers. Dr. Warner, who was a learned divine of the Established church, has given us but this one quarto of his general history of Ireland; but it comes not lower than the 12th century. He avows that difficulties did not affright him, yet it is said that he desisted from the

undertaking through disappointment in the parliamentary assistance, which his patron, the Duke of
Northumberland, had led him to expect.

16. 𝕷𝖊𝖑𝖆𝖓𝖉'𝖘 HISTORY OF IRELAND.
London, 1773. *3 vols. 4to.*

This book was highly praised on its first appearance, both for its style and matter ; strict investigation proves the former to be turgid—the latter
inaccurate. He has been censured for not making
more use of the abundant materials to be found in
the several record repositories of Ireland, and in
the public libraries of Great Britain. It affords,
however, a good general view of Irish affairs,
from the coming of the English to the Revolution.

17. 𝕻𝖑𝖔𝖜𝖉𝖊𝖓'𝖘 HISTORY OF IRELAND TO
THE UNION. *Lond.* 1803. *3 vols. 4to.*

This work may be considered as a useful continuation of Irish history, from the Revolution to
the Union ; but the author is not free from the
imputation of being a party writer. His partiality
to one class of the inhabitants of Ireland forms a
strong contrast with that of his cotemporary, Sir
Richard Musgrave, to the other ; of both the reader
may be told, " in medio tutissimus ibis." Mr.
Plowden appears to have been originally engaged
by the British ministry to compile a history of
Ireland : he complains, however, that, when the
work was completed, the author was neglected, in
consequence of writing with truth and impartiality.

18. **Nicholson's** Irish Historical Library. *Dublin,* 1724. *8vo.*

A valuable work, treating both of manuscript
and printed books relative to Ireland, as far as the
year 1700. It may be considered as the best preparatory book for the study of Irish history.

19. **Sir John Davies's** Discovery of
the true Causes why Ireland
was never entirely subdued.
London, 1612. *Small 4to.*

Bishop Nicholson, with great justice, calls this
book " the very best view of the political state of
" the kingdom, from the reign of Henry II. to
" that of James I." Sir J. D. was attorney-general
of Ireland in 1610. The many editions which his
work has gone through, and the frequent quota-
tions from it, are additional proofs of the high
esteem in which it has always been held. A MS.
copy, in the hand-writing of the time of James I.
(supposed to have been a presentation copy) and in
the original binding, is also in this collection.

20. An Account of **Ireland** in 1773,
by a late Chief Secretary of
that Kingdom. *8vo.*

Written by Sir George, afterwards Earl Macartney. It is a masterly sketch of the political history
of the country, and when viewed as a continuation

B

of Sir John Davies's work, both may be considered as forming an epitome of the political state of Ireland, from the landing of the English to Lord Townsend's administration, one of the striking epochs in the modern part of the history of the country.

21. Pacata Hibernia, *reprinted on imperial paper. Dublin*, 1810. *2 vols. 8vo.*

Written by Sir George Carew while president of Munster, under Queen Elizabeth. It contains the transactions of three years of much activity in Munster, from the latter end of 1599, to the death of the Queen.

22. Ancient Irish Histories. *Dublin*, 1809. *2 vols. Large paper. 8vo.*

A reprint of the works of the following ancient writers :—1st, Edmond Campion, who gives a slight account of the ancient history of Ireland, and of the English period, as far as the end of Sir Henry Sidney's government in 1571. 2d, Meredith Hanmer, who likewise couples the ancient and more modern periods, which he carries down no lower than 1284; but they are further continued by a very poor chronicle of Henry of Marlborough to the year 1421. These two pieces, together with Spencer's view of Ireland, in which are many excellent materials, were first published in small folio, by Sir James Ware, and put under the

patronage of the Lord Deputy Wentworth, in hopes
to excite others to make the public acquainted with
those scattered remains of the history of these
counties, which may help to fill up several chasms
in it.

23. 𝕳𝖆𝖗𝖗𝖎𝖘'𝖘 HIBERNICA; OR SOME AN-CIENT PIECES RELATING TO IRELAND. *Dublin*, 1757. *8vo.*

This interesting and valuable work consists of
two parts; the first contains Maurice Regan's
History; the Story of Rich. II. being last in Ireland;
the Voyage of Sir Richard Edgecomb, sent by
Hen. VII. into Ireland in 1488; the Breviate of
Baron Finglass in the reign of Hen. VIII. with
King Jas. I.'s project for the plantation of Ulster,
and several other papers connected with the settle-
ment of that part of Ireland; to which is added
an essay on the defects of the histories of Ireland,
addressed to the Lord Chancellor Newport, an
excellent performance of Walter Harris, the editor
of Ware. The second part consists of two treatises,
shewing how the laws and statutes of England became of force in Ireland.

24. 𝕷𝖔𝖉𝖌𝖊'𝖘 DESIDERATA CURIOSA HI-BERNICA. *Dublin*, 1772. *2 vols. 8vo.*

A collection of state papers, historical tracts, &c.
during the reigns of Elizabeth, Jas. I. and Char. I.

25. THE LIFE OF **O'Conor.** *Dublin, 8vo.*

This curious and very scarce volume is particularly valuable for the information it affords of the incipient steps taken by the Roman Catholics for the repeal of the penal laws. The first volume only was published, and was suppressed soon after it appeared, in consequence, as is supposed, of apprehensions that its circulation might injure the family. The second was committed to the flames before publication, at the author's particular request, by the friend to whose care it had been entrusted. A copy of the first volume went off, at a sale in Oxford, some years ago, for 14*l.*; the present copy was lately purchased at a sale in Dublin for 4*l.*

26. O'Conor's DISSERTATION ON THE ANCIENT HISTORY OF IRELAND, AND **O'Flaherty's** OGYGIA VINDICATED. *Dublin,* 1753, 1775. *2 vols. 8vo.*

The first edition of the dissertation. As the production of an Irish gentleman descended from one of the most respectable of the old Irish families, and deeply skilled in the language and written memorials of the history of this country, it ranks high in the scale of native literature. The author, who acknowledges the attentions of the celebrated Edmond Burke, impeaches in this work the authenticity of the poems attributed to Ossian, and charges

13

the translator with literary fraud and deception, in consequence of which it was afterwards attacked by many assailants. Mr. O'Conor has been emphatically called by General Vallancey, " the best Irish scholar that ever lived."

The second work in this volume, which is a vindication of some passages in the Ogygia, that had been attacked by Sir George Mackenzie, lay in MS. for many years after O'Flaherty's death, until published by Mr. O'Conor, who has prefixed a preliminary dissertation on the Antiquities of Ireland. The vindication is necessary for every person desirous of becoming acquainted with the early history and chronology of Ireland.

27. Vallancey's Collectanea. *Dublin,* 1781 *to* 1807. 6 *vols. 8vo.*

This useful compilation was commenced in 1774. Its original design was to bring into public notice scarce and unedited tracts relating to Ireland.— After the publication of a few numbers on this plan, it lay dormant, till the year 1781, when it was revived, chiefly at the instigation of the late Right Hon. William Burton Conyngham, who then instituted a society for the investigation of Irish antiquities. Some differences arising concerning colonization and etymology, the society dissolved: and the author of the Collectanea, with some trifling assistance from Mr. O'Conor of Balinagare, carried on the work nearly to the close of his life, but with a material deviation from the original design, for the latter numbers consist wholly of original disquisitions.

28. **Campbell's** STRICTURES ON THE ECCLESIASTICAL AND LITERARY HISTORY OF IRELAND. *Dublin,* 1789, 8*vo.*

This volume, which is very well written, and compiled with much ingenuity, is the work of the author of the Philosophical Survey of the South of Ireland. He was considered the most able assailant of the Milesian descent of the Irish ; but labouring under the disadvantage of a want of sufficient knowledge of the Irish language, he appears to have drawn many hasty and erroneous conclusions.— This work may not improperly be classed with Dr. Ledwich's Antiquities, as it combats the system of the late General Vallancey, but fails in the attempt to substitute another in its place. To this work is annexed, " An Historical Sketch of the Constitution and Government of Ireland, from the most early authenticated period, down to the year 1783 ; with an appendix." Both of them, however, appear to have been taken from Lord Macartney's Account of Ireland,* but very much disfigured and mutilated.

---

* See No. 20 of this Catalogue.

29. **Webb's** ANALYSIS OF THE HISTORY
AND ANTIQUITIES OF IRELAND.—
Dublin, 1791.

This writer steers a middle course between his
cotemporary and hostile system makers, Vallancey,
Ledwich, and Campbell, with each of whom he
dissents or agrees, as they appear to him correct or
otherwise. He inclines, however, to the antiquity
of Irish history, and his work bears the character
of being an elegant essay on the antiquities of the
country.

30. **Bishop of Down's** AND **Parson's**
DEFENCE OF THE ANCIENT HIS-
TORIANS AND HISTORY OF IRELAND.
Dublin, 1734 *and* 1794. *2 vols. in* 1.
8vo.

Two disquisitions on the credit to be given to
the writers on the early period of Irish history.—
The latter was written by Sir Lawrence Parsons,
now Earl of Rosse, in consequence of a bequest by
Henry Flood, Esq. to Trinity College, Dublin, for
founding a professorship of the Irish language.

31. **Columbanus** WITH **Plowden.** *3 vols.*

The letters of Columbanus were written by Dr.
Charles O'Conor, of Stowe, on the question of the
mode of appointing Roman Catholic bishops in
Ireland, and gave rise to a very warm and acrimo-
nious contest between him and Mr. Plowden. He

published seven letters under this assumed name. The third volume of this set contains Mr. Plowden's answer to Columbanus.

32. Parnell's HISTORICAL APOLOGY AND PENAL LAWS. *Dublin*, 1807 & 1808, *2 vols. 8vo.*

The first of these volumes contains a vindication of the Roman Catholics from the charges of disloyalty frequently brought against them since the Revolution. The authors were brothers, the former represented the County of Wicklow, the latter the Queen's County, in the Imperial Parliament.

33. Scully's PENAL LAWS. *Dub.* 1812. *3 parts in 1 vol. 8vo.*

A very able performance. The publisher was found guilty of a libel on the Duke of Richmond's administration, the matter of which is to be found in a note at page 229. The work itself consists of two parts: the third is in reality a kind of parody on the two former, written in a burlesque stile of imitation, to induce attention to it from the party whose tenets it was intended to overthrow.

34. STRICTURES ON Plowden's HISTORICAL REVIEW. *London*, 1804. *8vo.*

Evidently written by Sir Richard Musgrave, the author of the history of the rebellion in 1798. At

least Plowden, who terms Sir Richard "a stipen‑
diary scavenger of slanderous untruths," has an‑
swered him in An Historical Letter.

35. 𝔐ountmorres on the Irish Par‑ liament. *London*, 1792. *2 vols. 8vo.*

This work is not a parliamentary history, even of
the period from 1633 to 1666, of which it professes
to treat, but rather imperfect collections; for several
tracts bearing but slightly on the subject, are inserted
at full length, extracts of which might have been
given with more propriety. These collections are,
however, valuable, instructive, and amusing. The
appendix to it contains a translation of Gir. Cam‑
brensis's account of the invasion of Ireland, and a
life of the first duke of Ormond.

36. 𝔉alkland's Review of the Irish House of Commons ; and on Par‑ liamentary Representation. *Dub‑ lin*, 1789, 1790. *2 vols. in one. 8vo.*

The first part of this book consists of a curious
and interesting review of the characters of the
leading members of the Irish House of Commons,
shortly previous to the Union; the second is a
review of the representation, particularly that of the
boroughs. It is said to have been written by a literary
gentleman, of the name of Scott, then better known
by the title of Beau Myrtle.

37. 𝔓𝔬𝔲=𝔯𝔬𝔲, OR AN HISTORICAL AND CRITICAL INQUIRY INTO THE PHYSIOLOGY AND PATHOLOGY OF PARLIAMENTS. *Dublin,* 1786. *8vo.*

A most eccentric production, yet abounding with curious and useful information on the subjects of legislation and government.

38. 𝔐𝔬𝔯𝔶𝔰𝔬𝔫'𝔰 HISTORY AND DESCRIPTION OF IRELAND. *Dublin,* 1735. *2 vols. 8vo.*

Fynes Moryson was secretary to Lord Mountjoy, lord deputy of Ireland during the last years of the reign of Elizabeth. These volumes are taken from his Itinerary, published in folio. They contain a brief exposé of the general history of the country, from the first landing of the English till his own times, on which he dwells largely. ☞ This work should have been placed after the Pacata Hibernia, as it refers to the same period.

☞ The period of the Union of Great Britain and Ireland has been fixed on as the termination of the Historical department of this Collection. It is the commencement of a new era, which could not well be entered upon, without departing from the principle that forms the basis of a Select Library. To this may be added, that the possessor of this Library has already a very extensive collection of Tracts on Irish affairs, and more particularly on those of the period here referred to.

BIOGRAPHY.

39. **Carte's** LIFE OF THE DUKE OF OR-
MOND, AND LETTERS. *London*, 1735,
1736. *3 vols. folio.*

This work, which is incomplete without the letters,
affords a clear and satisfactory view of Irish affairs
during the life of the great duke, who took a leading
part in most of the transactions of those times. He
was born in 1610, and died in 1684. Walter Harris
has said, " that the author has met with the hard fate
" of pleasing neither party, while the papists think
" he has borne too severe upon them, and the protes-
" tants are of opinion he has favoured the popish
" cause too much." A collection of original letters
and papers concerning the affairs of England from
1640 to 1660, found among the duke of Ormond's
papers, was published by Carte in 1739. They are
said to have been printed at the expense of the
Society for the Encouragement of Learning. None
of them are to be found in the folio edition of the
letters attached to Carte's Life of Ormond.

40. **Hardy's** LIFE OF THE EARL OF CHAR-
LEMONT. *London*, 1812. *2 vols. 8vo.*

These volumes relate more to the public than to
the private life of the Earl of Charlemont, and

contain much useful information on the history of Ireland, from the period of the octennial parliaments to the union. The author was a member of the Irish house of commons during part of that period, and, therefore, well informed as to many of the facts. It is said, that he was assisted in the compilation of the work by Mr. Grattan. ☞ This work has also been published in Quarto.

41. LIFE OF 𝔖𝔦𝔯 𝔍𝔬𝔥𝔫 𝔓𝔢𝔯𝔯𝔬𝔱𝔱. *London,* 1728. *8vo.*

This work, which was published from an original document, written about the end of the reign of Elizabeth, in some measure supplies the historical defects in that reign, as it contains much information relative to Ireland, during the time that this unfortunate statesman held the reins of government there.

42. 𝔏𝔬𝔡𝔤𝔢'𝔰 PEERAGE OF IRELAND, BY 𝔄𝔯𝔠𝔥𝔡𝔞𝔩𝔩. *Dublin,* 1788. 7 *vols.* *8vo.*

The first edition of the Irish peerage was originally compiled and published in four volumes, by John Lodge, esq. who was deputy-keeper of the rolls in Ireland. The present edition is an enlargement and continuation of it, by the Rev. Mervyn Archdall, author of the Monasticon Hibernicum.

43. Memoirs of the Family of 𝕲𝖗𝖆𝖈𝖊,
   by Sheffield Grace, Esq. f. s. a.
   London, 1823. 8*vo*.

This volume, which is intended solely for private
distribution, contains not only a general memoir of
the Grace family, but also of several of its most
celebrated branches. Then follows a poem on Jer-
point Abbey, the ancient burial place of the family,
two genealogical tables, and a collection of monumental inscriptions, and other commemorative compositions. These memoirs, which are finely printed,
and illustrated with upwards of fifty engravings,
form the most curious account extant in print of
any private family in the kingdom. Some historical
facts, taken from original documents, and not to
be found elsewhere, are also given in this interesting volume.

TOPOGRAPHY.

44. **Beaufort's** MEMOIR OF THE MAP OF IRELAND, AND **Propert's** TOPOGRAPHICAL TABLE. *London,* 1792, *and Dublin,* 1808. 4*to.*

The memoir was written to accompany a map constructed by the author, exhibiting the ecclesiastical state of Ireland, and contains much geographical and topographical information. Propert's work is an account of the principal seaports in the British islands, illustrated by a map descriptive of the coasts ; it contains some statistical information respecting each.

45. **Seward's** TOPOGRAPHIA HIBERNICA. *Dublin,* 1795. 4*to.*

A valuable topographical dictionary, particularly as to the civil state of the country, abounding with historical and antiquarian notices. ☞ A pocket edition was also printed in 1789.

46. **Carlisle's** TOPOGRAPHICAL DICTIONARY OF IRELAND. *Dub.* 1810. 4*to.*

A useful book of reference, chiefly compiled from the ecclesiastical returns made to parliament in 1805-7.

47. **Whitelaw** AND **Walsh's** HISTORY
OF THE CITY OF DUBLIN. *London,*
1810. 4*to.*

This work was commenced by John Warburton,
esq. deputy keeper of the records in Birmingham
Tower, as an enlargement of Harris's History of
Dublin, and continued by the Rev. James Whitelaw,
vicar of St. Catherine's, Dublin, on a more extended
plan. On this gentleman's death, it was taken up,
and concluded by the Rev. Robert Walsh. It deserves rather the name of a mine of materials, than
of a regular history, as it is very deficient in ar-
rangement and method.

48. **Monck Mason's** HISTORY OF THE
CATHEDRALS. *Dublin,* 1820. 4*to.*

The first part only of this elaborate work is published, comprising the history of the cathedral of
St. Patrick's, Dublin. It displays much antiquarian
research, and contains a very able defence of the
character of dean Swift against the attacks of Sir
Walter Scott and the Edinburgh Reviewers, in the
course of which much curious matter relative to
this illustrious Irish patriot and author is introduced.

49. **Hardiman's** HISTORY OF GALWAY.
Dublin, 1820. 4*to.*

This is also an elaborate performance, and a valuable addition to Irish topography. The author,

who is a native of Galway, and appears to have
entered upon his work *con amore*, was eminently
qualified for its execution, from his employment
under the Board of Public Records in Ireland ; the
stores of which he has sedulously investigated, and
judiciously applied to elucidate his subject.—
Both this and the preceding work are favorable
specimens of the improvement of typography in
Dublin.

50. Boate's AND Molyneaux's NATU-RAL HISTORY OF IRELAND. *Dublin,* 1755. 4*to.*

The natural history of Ireland was written by
Dr. Gerard Boate, and published after his death, in
1652, in small 8vo. by his brother, Dr. Arnold
Boate, who resided in Dublin as a physician. It
was re-edited and enlarged by Molyneaux in 1726,
and re-printed in 1755. The work contains also a
a discourse on the Danish mounts, forts, and round
towers in Ireland, written by Molyneaux.

51. Barton's LECTURES ON LOUGH-NEAGH. *Dublin,* 1751. 4*to.*

A course of lectures on mineralogy and geology,
intended as an introduction to the natural history
of several counties contiguous to Lough Neagh. It
contains also an account of the lake of Killarney.

52. **Poole** AND **Cash's** VIEWS OF THE
PUBLIC BUILDINGS IN DUBLIN.——
Dublin, 1780. 4*to*.

This volume, which is the joint production of
two artists, becomes every day more interesting, as
affording to those who visit Dublin the means of
comparing what this beautiful city then was, with
what it is at present, and thus tracing the progress
of its architectural improvement. It is now scarce.
A perfect copy should contain plans of Dublin in
1610 and 1780.

53. **Harris's** HISTORY OF DUBLIN. *Dublin*, 1766. 8*vo*.

A posthumous work, compiled from the author's
papers, but very inferior to his other productions.

54. **Harris's** ANCIENT AND PRESENT
STATE OF THE COUNTY OF DOWN.
Dublin, 1757. 8*vo*.

This was done by Walter Harris and Dr. Lyons,
and was the first work published under the auspices
of the Physico-Historical Society, a literary asso-
ciation, formed in Dublin about the year 1744, with
a view of removing the gross misrepresentations
which had been handed down from early ages concerning the country.

55. 𝕾𝖒𝖎𝖙𝖍'𝖘 Ancient and Present State of the County of Water-ford. *Dublin*, 1746. *8vo.*

The author of this, and the two following works, was one of the earliest and most active members of the Physico-Historical Society. His History of Waterford, which was the first of the series of county histories written by him, was presented to that society in 1745, and immediately printed under its sanction. Both it and the subsequent work were re-printed in 1774.

56. 𝕾𝖒𝖎𝖙𝖍'𝖘 Ancient and Present State of the County and City of Cork. *Dublin*, 1749. *8vo.*

The history of Cork is the most extended, and best executed of this writer's works. A third edition has been lately published in Cork.

57. 𝕾𝖒𝖎𝖙𝖍'𝖘 History of the County of Kerry. *Dublin*, 1756. *8vo.*

Doctor O'Conor speaks of this as being rather materials than history. It is the scarcest of Smith's works. To it is added a tract of Vallancey's (not included in his Collectanea) describing the ruins of an amphitheatre in Kerry.

58. **Ferrar's** HISTORY OF LIMERICK.
   Limerick, 1787. *8vo.*

The author was an inhabitant of Limerick; his character, as a writer on topography, is not high.

59. **Hamilton's** LETTERS CONCERNING THE NORTHERN COAST OF ANTRIM.
   Dublin, 1790. *8vo.*

Hamilton was a fellow of Trinity College, Dublin, and took an active part in the Neptunian and Volcanian controversy. His work is much esteemed and sought after, as an entertaining and instructive guide, not only to the natural history, but to the customs, manners, and antiquities of that interesting part of the island. It has passed through several editions. The last, printed in Belfast, with an Itinerary to the Giant's Causeway, by M'Skimin, the author of the following work, is the best.

60. **M'Skimin's** HISTORY OF CARRICKFERGUS. *Belfast, 1811.* *12mo.*

The compilation of a working weaver in Carrickfergus, executed with intelligence and industry.

☞ An edition in octavo has been lately published, which may justly be called a new work, in consequence of its numerous additions and improvements. Those who wish to make themselves acquainted with the state of the North of Ireland, the theatre of so many important events, particularly during the reigns of Elizabeth and Charles I. will gain much information by consulting the new edition of this work.

61. 𝔖tewart's History of Armagh. *Newry, 1819. 8vo.*

This work gives a full and impartial view of many of the great events of Irish history with which the city of Armagh was directly or incidentally connected. The author engages in the Ledwicherian controversy as to St. Patrick, in which, contrary to that learned writer's opinion, he maintains the existence of the favourite saint of the city whose annals he has compiled.

62. Historical Collections relative to the Town of 𝔅elfast. *Belfast, 1817. 8vo.*

A meagre collection of annals chiefly compiled, particularly as to its modern materials, from the newspapers and other periodical publications, but useful as a book of reference.

63. The Present State of 𝔍reland. *London, 1673. 12mo.*

This is a scarce and valuable little tract, whether considered in an historical, political, or statistical point of view. It contains a short sketch of the history of Ireland; a detailed account of its topographical divisions and a description of its chief towns. The author's name is unknown. Prefixed to it is a curious map of Ireland.

64. 𝕽𝖚𝖙𝖙𝖞'𝖘 NATURAL HISTORY OF THE COUNTY DUBLIN. *Dublin,* 1772. *8vo.*

The author of this work was an ingenious and learned quaker that practiced physic in Dublin. In the preface he informs us, that he undertook the work at the request of the Physico-Historical Society, at the head of which then was Lord Chancellor Newport.

65. 𝕽𝖚𝖙𝖙𝖞'𝖘 HISTORY OF THE WEATHER AND SEASONS, AND OF THE PREVAILING DISEASES IN DUBLIN. *London,* 1770. *8vo.*

A writer in the Anthologia Hibernica observes, that this work does great honour to Dr. Rutty as a physician and accurate meteorologist.

66. 𝕽𝖚𝖙𝖙𝖞 ON MINERAL WATERS. *Dublin,* 1757. *8vo.*

The synopsis of mineral waters was examined soon after its publication, and censured, by the celebrated Irish patriot, Dr. Lucas, in his Analysis of the Synopsis. Lucas was a much better chymist than Rutty; however, the latter replied in an Examination of the Analysis.

67. 𝕻𝖆𝖙𝖙𝖊𝖗𝖘𝖔𝖓 ON THE CLIMATE OF IRELAND. *Dublin,* 1804. *8vo.*

Taken chiefly from observations made in Londonderry in 1801. It contains also thoughts on some branches of rural economy, particularly planting, and the Linen Manufacture.

68. **Griffith's** GEOLOGICAL AND MINING SURVEYS. *Dublin*, 1814, 1818. *2 vols. 8vo.*

These surveys are published in the form of reports to the Dublin Society, to which the author is mining engineer. They contain chiefly an investigation of the districts in Leinster and Connaught, where traces have been discovered of coal, a mineral the want of which is severely felt in most parts of Ireland.

69. **Richardson's** ESSAY ON FIORIN, AND **White** ON THE INDIGENOUS GRASSES OF IRELAND. *Dublin*, 1808. *8vo.*

Doctor Richardson, who had been a fellow of Trinity College, Dublin, distinguished himself during the later period of his life, as a writer on agriculture, and more particularly by his indefatigable exertions to introduce into notice the qualities of a species of grass, called by the natives Fiorin. White was under-gardener in the Botanic Garden of the Dublin Society. His treatise consists of a systematic catalogue of the grasses, with their descriptions and leading properties. To each is annexed its Irish appellation, an addition that adds much to the practical utility of his book.

STATISTICAL SURVEYS.

70. **Wakefield's** STATISTICAL AND PO-
LITICAL ACCOUNT OF IRELAND.——
London, 1809. *2 vols. 4to.*

The late bishop of Waterford, Dr. Stock, called
these volumes, "two ponderous quartos, stuffed
"with important errors." The work may be beyond
the ability of one man to execute well, but it contains much useful information on Ireland.

71. **Newenham's** VIEW OF THE NATU-
RAL, POLITICAL AND COMMERCIAL
CIRCUMSTANCES OF IRELAND. *London*,
1809. *4to.*

This work, by the author of the essay on the
population of Ireland, was written under a persua-
sion that there was a general defect of information
relative to Ireland, and is designed to correct this
error. It therefore commences by pointing out the
natural advantages of the island for the acquire-
ment of commercial wealth, and the causes by
which these have been frustrated. The author has
collected a mass of historical and statistical information, very useful, but not altogether free from
the high colouring which men are apt to give to
a favorite subject.

72. **Young's** Tour in Ireland. *London,*
    1780. *4to.*

This work, the result of several years researches
through the country, may be considered as the first,
and among the best of the treatises on the agricultural state of Ireland. The author's remarks on
the inexpediency of bounties on the inland carriage
of corn were acted upon ; and hence may be dated
the commencement of extended tillage in Ireland.
He pointed out strongly the prejudicial effects of
the penal code on the industry of the people ; he
also foresaw the benefits of a legislative union, and
lived to see many of the effects resulting from the
adoption of both those suggestions.

73. **Fraser's** Review of the Fisheries
    of Great Britain and Ireland.
    Edinb. 1818. *4to.*

By the author of the Statistical Surveys of the
two maritime counties of Wexford and Wicklow.
It gives a full account of the attempts made during
the last century to encourage the Irish fisheries,
and the causes of their failure.

COUNTY SURVEYS, **Describing** 21 **Counties.**

These surveys were published under the patronage, and partly at the expense, of the Dublin
Society, to whom an additional parliamentary grant

was made for the purpose. In some instances they appear to have been imperfectly executed, and do not afford the information that might have been expected from their mode of publication. There are, however, some splendid exceptions to this remark, particularly in the surveys of Cork, Kilkenny, and Londonderry.

74. Antrim. *Dublin,* 1812. *8vo.*

By the Rev. John Dubourdieu, rector of Annahilt, in the diocese of Down, inscribed to General Vallancey.

75. Armagh. *Dublin,* 1804. *8vo.*

By Sir Charles Coote, Bart. dedicated to the Right Honorable John Foster.

76. Cavan. *Dublin,* 1802. *8vo.*

By Sir Charles Coote, Bart. with a dedication to the Earl of Hardwicke.

77. Cork. *Dublin,* 1810. *8vo.*

By the Rev. Horatio Townsend, a clergyman in the diocese of Cork and Ross, with a dedication to the Earl of Shannon.

78. Clare. *Dublin,* 1808. *8vo.*

By Heley Dutton, with a preface, but no dedication.

79. **Donegal.** *Dublin,* 1802. 8*vo.*

By James M'Pharlan, M. D. dedicated to General Vallancey.

80. **Down.** *Dublin,* 1802. 8*vo.*

By the Rev. John Dubourdieu, with preliminary observations.

81. **Dublin.** *Dublin,* 1802. 8*vo.*

By Lieutenant Joseph Archer, to which is added Dutton's observations on Archer's Survey, dedicated to Lieutenant General Vallancey.

82. **Kilkenny.** *Dublin,* 1802. 8*vo.*

By William Tighe of Woodstock, near Inistiogue, in the County of Kilkenny, esq. This valuable volume is stiled " Statistical Observations," and is inscribed by the author to the Dublin Society.

83. **King's** AND **Queen's Counties.** *Dublin,* 1801. *2 vols. in one.* 8*vo.*

Both by Sir Charles Coote, Bart. They appear to be the first two volumes of the County Surveys; the former is dedicated to Lieut. Gen. Vallancey, and the latter to the Right Hon. John Foster.

84. 𝕶𝖎𝖑𝖉𝖆𝖗𝖊.   *Dublin,* 1807.   *8vo.*

By Thomas James Rawson, esq. with a preface, but no dedication.

85. 𝕷𝖊𝖎𝖙𝖗𝖎𝖒, 𝕸𝖆𝖞𝖔, AND 𝕾𝖑𝖎𝖌𝖔.——
Dublin, 1802.   *3 vols. in one.*   *8vo.*

By James M'Pharlan, M. D.   These three surveys are but slight sketches of the subject; that of Mayo is inscribed to the Marquess of Sligo.

86. 𝕷𝖔𝖓𝖉𝖔𝖓𝖉𝖊𝖗𝖗𝖞.   *Dublin,* 1802.   *8vo.*

By the Rev. George Vaughan Sampson, rector of Aghanlooe, in the diocese of Derry, inscribed to General Vallancey.

87. 𝕸𝖊𝖆𝖙𝖍.   *Dublin,* 1802.   *8vo.*

By Robert Thompson, esq. of Oatlands, with a short historical introduction.   This is the scarcest of all the Surveys.

88. 𝕸𝖔𝖓𝖆𝖌𝖍𝖆𝖓.   *Dublin,* 1801.   *8vo.*

By Sir Charles Coote, Bart. with an historical introduction, and a dedication to Richard Dawson, esq. representative for the county of Monaghan.

89. **Tyrone.** *Dublin,* 1802. *8vo.*

By John M'Evoy, with a dedication to Viscount Mountjoy.

90. **Wexford** AND **Wicklow.** *Dublin,* 1801. *2 vols. in one. 8vo.*

By Robert Frazer, esq. author of some valuable agricultural reports in England. He has written since on the Fisheries of Great Britain and Ireland, as noticed in a former part of the Catalogue.

91. **Shaw Mason's** PAROCHIAL SURVEYS, OR STATISTICAL ACCOUNT OF IRELAND. *Dublin,* 1814 - 16 - 19.— *3 vols. 8vo.*

This work is chiefly drawn up from the communications of the clergy : it originated under the auspices of the RIGHT HON. ROBERT PEEL, while in the government of Ireland, and is designed to give a minute statistical account of the several districts in the country ; each parish forming a distinct section. In addition to the local information thus afforded, each volume is enriched by an introductory essay on some point connected with the general subject. In the first is a Synopsis of political economy ; in the second, an Analysis of the Down Survey ; and in the third, an Essay on the population of Ireland.

92. Survey, Valuation, and Census of the Barony of Portnehinch, compiled, in the year 1819, by W. Shaw Mason, esq. m. r. i. a. Dublin, 1821. 1 vol. folio.

" It is obvious," observes Sir John Sinclair in his General Report of Scotland, " that no indivi-
" dual can rationally undertake to improve his
" landed property, without knowing its extent, the
" soil of which it consists, the number of farmers
" by whom it is occupied, the state of the build-
" ings erected upon it, the crops which it is capable
" of producing, the best means of cultivating it,
" &c. In the same manner, no government can
" improve a country, or ameliorate the condition
" of its inhabitants, without entering into minute
" inquiries of a similar nature, for the purpose of
" at least removing all obstacles to improvement."
Influenced by the truth of this position, the author of the preceding work took advantage of the KING's late visit to Ireland, to lay before His Majesty the " Survey of Portnehinch," as a model for carrying into effect a General Survey and Valuation of the whole of the country, under the name of the " Royal Statistical Survey of Ireland." The following inscription prefixed to the work, affords a concise, yet clear view of the design and objects to be attained :—

THE FOLLOWING SURVEY OF A BARONY,
INTENDED AS A MODEL FOR
A ROYAL STATISTICAL SURVEY OF
IRELAND,
AND DESIGNED, LIKE DOOMSDAY BOOK,
BY A MINUTE INQUIRY INTO
THE CAPABILITIES AND RESOURCES OF THE COUNTRY,
TO LAY THE FOUNDATION OF ITS
PERMANENT PROSPERITY AND HAPPINESS;
THUS HANDING DOWN TO FUTURE AGES,
A RECORD OF WISDOM AND BENEFICENCE IN AN

ENLIGHTENED AND BELOVED MONARCH,

ON HIS FIRST APPROACH TO ITS SHORES TO RECEIVE
THE GREETINGS OF A LOYAL AND AFFECTIONATE PEOPLE,
IS MOST HUMBLY SUBMITTED
TO THE KING'S MOST EXCELLENT MAJESTY,
BY HIS DEVOTED AND FAITHFUL
SUBJECT AND SERVANT,

W. S. M.

RECORD TOWER,
DUBLIN CASTLE.
AUGUST, 1821.

93. **Petty's** POLITICAL TRACTS, CHIEFLY
RELATING TO IRELAND. *Dublin,*
1769. AND REFLECTIONS ON MEN
AND THINGS IN IRELAND. *Ibid.* 2
vols. in one. 8vo.

The celebrated author of these tracts had
superintended the great territorial Survey of Ireland, instituted during the Protectorate for the
distribution of forfeited property. Bishop Nichol-

son observes, that " he obliged the learned part of mankind with the Political Anatomy of Ireland," one of the tracts contained in this volume, and certainly one of the first and most valuable statistical documents respecting the country. The bishop also adds, that " he wrote choice observations on the Dublin bills of mortality, baptisms, and burials, houses, hearths, &c. which will be of lasting use to all that shall have the curiosity hereafter to consider the gradual improvement of that great city." The tract thus spoken of is mentioned in this volume as a treatise of taxes and contributions. Then follow his essays on political Arithmetic, and lastly the political Anatomy of Ireland, already mentioned. To this edition is prefixed " The last will of that great master of political arithmetic, Sir William Petty, knight, founder of the noble family of Shelburn," now represented by the Marquess of Lansdowne.— " The Reflections" is a defence of his conduct against some attacks made upon him in the Irish house of commons, by Sir Jerome Sankey.

94. **Newenham** ON THE POPULATION OF IRELAND ; AND **Whitelaw** ON THE POPULATION OF DUBLIN. *London, 1805, and Dublin, 1805. 2 vols. in one. 8vo.*

The writer of the former of these essays is also author of several valuable tracts on Ireland. His chief objects in the present appear to be, to point out the defective basis upon which all previous attempts to ascertain the population of Ireland rested; to show the rapid increase of the inhabitants, particularly during the last century; to ascertain the number actually living in Ireland at the period of the publication of this treatise; and to prove the capability of the country to support a much greater population than it then maintained. The train of argument is ingenious, and well supported.

The peculiar circumstances of the city of Dublin during the rebellion of 1798, led Mr. Whitelaw (one of the joint authors of the History of Dublin, already noticed) to undertake an account of the population by actual enumeration. At that period, every householder was obliged to affix, on the outside of his door, a list of the names of every person then residing in it. The numbers were thence collected by Mr. Whitelaw, and published by him; together with a comparative statement of the numbers, taken in 1803, by the conservators of the peace, after the insurrection in that year.

TOURISTS.

95. **Weld's** KILLARNEY. *London,* 1807.
4*to.*

A book that should form part of the travelling
equipage of every visitor to these romantic scenes.
The descriptions are accurate, well selected, and
enlivened by judicious remarks and anecdotes.—
The views of the lake scenery, which constitute no
small part of the value of the volume, are well
chosen, and executed in a masterly style, both as
to drawing and engraving.

96. **Sir John Carr's** STRANGER IN
IRELAND. *London,* 1806. 4*to.*

This volume, which forms a large quarto, deserves rather the name of a tourist's common-place
book, than a tour. Instead of arranging his materials, so as to present his reader with an elegant
selection of novelties, he serves them a feast of stale
jests and fulsome compliments. In style he is both
careless and affected; sentences sometimes without
meaning, and sometimes without grammar—high-
flown descriptions, neither prose nor poetry, often
terminating in nothing. The work however contains many facts and observations relative to the
country and its inhabitants, worthy of notice. The
writer's range was chiefly through the southern
parts of Ireland.

97. 𝕸𝖎𝖘𝖘 𝕻𝖑𝖚𝖒𝖙𝖗𝖊𝖊'𝖘 NARRATIVE OF A RESIDENCE IN IRELAND. *London*, 1817. 4*to*.

This volume exhibits many of the characteristic features of Sir John Carr's previous work, and those enlarged to a greater degree of caricatura: it is, like his, a large quarto, abounding with anecdotes of persons whom few know, and descriptions that few can read through; like his also, some information respecting the country, though much less both as to quantity and quality, and much more distorted by prejudice and misinformation, can be gleaned from it. This lady's literary evil genius led her through most parts of the country.

98. 𝕯𝖚𝖓𝖙𝖔𝖓'𝖘 DUBLIN SCUFFLE. *Dublin*, 1699. 8*vo*.

This eccentric production may be considered as the earliest attempt at Irish topography. The present copy had been in Bishop Stock's library, and contains some bibliographical memoranda, in his lordship's hand-writing. Pope has preserved the memory of Dunton in the following lines of the Dunciad:

> With that she gave him (piteous of his case,
> Yet smiling at his rueful length of face)
> A shaggy tap'stry, worthy to be spread
> On Codrus' old, or Dunton's modern bed.

Book ii. *line* 133.

See also **Pope's Note** on this passage.

99. Chetwood's Tour through Ireland, *London*, 1748. *8vo.*

The oldest of the tourists, except Dunton, who visited Ireland in 1699. Though stiled A Tour through Ireland, it is confined to the south-eastern counties, commencing with Cork, proceeding northwards, and terminating with the author's arrival in the city of Dublin.

100. Bushe's Hibernia Curiosa. *London*, 1764. *8vo.*

This work embraces nearly the same tract of country as the preceding, being the account of a journey from Dublin to Killarney. It also gives a description of the Giant's Causeway. The print of an Irish car, in p. 25, though very badly executed, is not uncharacteristic.

101. Derrick's Letters. *Dublin*, 1767. *8vo.*

The author of these letters was master of the ceremonies at Bath. Like the two former tours, it is chiefly confined to the eastern and southern parts of Ireland. At the conclusion are two letters from William Ockendon, esq. M. P. for Great Marlow, giving a description of the Lake of Killarney. They were all written about the year 1760.

102. **Twiss'** Tour in Ireland in 1775. *Dublin*, 1776. 12*mo*.

The author of this tour has been "damned to everlasting fame" for some severe remarks on the Irish ladies. Though the range of country described in it extends from north to south, the small size of the volume affords but little scope for valuable detail.

103. **Elstob's** Trip to Kilkenny, from Durham, by way of Whitehaven and Dublin, in the year 1766. 12*mo*.

Contains many curious particulars respecting the manners of the lower classes of the Irish, related as they affected the writer, who seems to have been from the north of England. His tour is confined to part of Leinster.

104. **Campbell's** Philosophical Survey of the South of Ireland. *Dublin*, 1778. 8*vo*.

Written by Dr. Campbell, author of the Strictures on the Ecclesiastical History of Ireland.—This tour extends from Dublin to Cork, and the author has been always considered as among the best of the Irish tourists. It contains several interesting notices and disquisitions on the national antiquities, and on the political state of the country.

105. **Luckomb's** Tour through Ireland. *London,* 1783. *8vo.*

The work comprehends four tours made through the four quarters of the island. It is written in a plain and rather homely style, but indicates much observation and sound sense in the writer.

106. **Bowden's** Tour through Ireland. *Dublin,* 1791. *12mo.*

This tourist's observations extend to every quarter of the country, but they contain little to interest or instruct.

107. **Holmes's** Tour in Ireland in 1799. *8vo.*

The author entitles his book " Sketches of some " of the Southern Counties of Ireland, taken in the " year 1797." They are but slight sketches, chiefly taken in the south-western counties, and are illustrated by several well executed engravings.

108. **Cooper's** Letters on the Irish Nation in the Year 1799. *London,* 1801. *8vo.*

These letters contain many interesting observations on the political state of Ireland at the eventful period of the Union. The work has gone through a second edition.

109. **Latocnay**, PROMENADE DU FRAN-
COIS DANS L'IRLANDE.   *a Brunswick,*
1801.   8*vo.*

The author was a native of France, who made a
pedestrian tour through the greatest part of Ireland.
The narrative is lively and amusing.

110. **Milner's** ENQUIRY.   *London,* 1808.
8*vo.*

The chief points noticed in this tour, which
extends through the southern counties, are the state
of the Roman Catholics, and the architectural antiquities of the country. He enters the lists against
Dr. Ledwich, in defence of the tutelar saint of
Ireland.

111. **Hoare's** JOURNAL OF A TOUR IN
IRELAND.   *London,* 1810.   8*vo.*

By the celebrated antiquarian ; to it is prefixed
an introductory discourse on the ancient history of
Ireland, about the period of the landing of the
English, which occupies no small part of the volume.
The tour itself is less interesting to the general
reader than to the lover of antiquities, though
even those will regret the want of engravings to
elucidate the writer's descriptions.

112. 𝕯𝖊𝖜𝖆𝖗'𝖘 OBSERVATIONS ON THE IRISH. *London,* 1812. *8vo.*

The avowed object of the inquiries of this author, who is a native of Scotland, was to improve the condition of the great body of the people of Ireland. His observations on this interesting subject breath a spirit of kindly affection, highly creditable to the writer. His remarks upon the advantages of the general diffusion of education are particularly worthy of notice.

113. 𝕲𝖆𝖒𝖇𝖑𝖊'𝖘 SKETCHES IN 1812, AND VIEW OF SOCIETY AND MANNERS IN 1814, IN DUBLIN, AND THE NORTH OF IRELAND. *London,* 1811 & 1813. 2 *vols. in one.* 8vo.

A work abounding in entertaining anecdote, to be perused with some caution, as the author is thought to have allowed his imagination at times to take excursions at the expense of truth.

114. 𝕳𝖆𝖑𝖑'𝖘 TOUR THROUGH IRELAND. *London,* 1813. *8vo.*

Written by a Scotch clergyman, who visited the country for the express purpose of making himself acquainted with the national peculiarities, by mixing among the natives of every rank. His tour, which extends through all parts of the island, abounds in minute detail and anecdote relative to the lower classes.

115. An Englishman's Tour in Ireland in the years 1813 and 1814. *Dublin,* 1816. *8vo.*

A plain matter of fact narrative, written by a member of the society of Friends, of what the author saw and collected during a tour through a great part of Ireland. It is confined to the southern and eastern parts.

116. Atkinson's Irish Tourist. *Dublin,* 1815. *8vo.*

This volume seems to have been a laborious compilation, apparently the work of a man who has seen what he describes, and hence it contains a good deal of local information relative to the parts of the country he visited.

117. Lord Blaney's Sequel to a Narrative, with Observations on the present State of Ireland. *London,* 1816. *8vo.*

Lord Blaney had published the narrative of a tour through Spain and France from 1810 to 1814, to which he has appended these observations as an additional volume, though connected with them by no other clue than that of the author's personal identity. As a tourist he could not be omitted in a collection professing to give a complete view of Irish topographical writers; but the notes of his journey seemed designed as pegs, on which to hang political disquisitions, rather than as a delineation of the features of the country.

118. Curwen's OBSERVATIONS ON THE STATE OF IRELAND. *London*, 1818. 2 *vols.* 8*vo.*

The observations of this author, who is the celebrated English agriculturist, are chiefly directed to illustrate his favorite pursuit. The letters were the result of a hasty tour through the island, in the year 1815, but were not published until 1818, in consequence of a parliamentary discussion relative to the comparative situation of the labouring classes in the two islands, in which the author took a leading part.

119. The Scientific Tourist THROUGH IRELAND. *London*, 1818. 12*mo.*

A compilation for the use of travellers, well digested, and arrranged according to counties.

120. Trotter's WALKS THROUGH IRELAND. *London*, 1819. 8*vo.*

A posthumous work of Mr. J. Bernard Trotter, private secretary to Charles James Fox, and author of the memoir of that celebrated character, and other works. The observations in these " Walks" indicate an elegant and instructed mind, strongly tinctured with the spirit of romance. A well written memoir of the author is prefixed.

FINANCE.

121 **Clarendon's** Sketch of the Revenue and Finance of Ireland. *London,* 1791. 4*to.*

This publication, to use the author's own words, may be considered as a collection and digest of various financial statements, which, while it aims at giving a sketch of the Irish revenue, may furnish materials to form an extensive history of the subject.

122. **Cavendish** on the Public Accounts of Ireland. *London,* 1791. 8*vo.*

A work compiled from the public accounts laid before parliament every session, and published for the use of the younger members. It consists wholly of figures.

123. **Hutchinson's** Commercial Restraints of Ireland Considered. *Dublin,* 1779. 8*vo.*

The author of this tract was the celebrated John Hely Hutchinson, provost of Trinity College, Dublin, and well known among the political characters that flourished in Ireland before the Union.

The object of the treatise is to prove, that the distresses of Ireland chiefly proceeded from the ill-judged restraints imposed upon its commerce by Great Britain, and particularly from the destruction of its Woollen Trade, which was effected during the reign of King William. It contains much powerful argument, and many strong pictures of the state of the country, antecedent to, and during the time of which the author treats.

124. 𝕮𝖍𝖆𝖑𝖒𝖊𝖗'𝖘 HISTORICAL VIEW OF THE DOMESTIC ECONOMY OF GREAT BRITAIN˙ AND IRELAND. *Edinburgh*, 1812. 8vo.

This valuable work contains one chapter on the state of Ireland, which takes a concise but masterly view of its political and commercial progress, from the reign of James I. to the Union. This chapter is not in the first edition, published in 1804.

125. 𝕷𝖆𝖜𝖗𝖊𝖓𝖈𝖊'𝖘 INTEREST OF IRELAND. *Dublin*, 1682. 18mo.

The trade and wealth of Ireland are stated in two parts, by Colonel Richard Lawrence, who was many years member of the Council of Trade, as well as an officer of rank in the army.

FINIS.